INFELICIA.

INFELICIA

By

Adah Isaacs Menken

The Black Heritage Library Collection

BOOKS FOR LIBRARIES PRESS
FREEPORT, NEW YORK
1971

First Published 1868
Reprinted 1971

PS 2389
M24

Reprinted from a copy in the
Fisk University Library Negro Collection

INTERNATIONAL STANDARD BOOK NUMBER:
0-8369-8928-7

LIBRARY OF CONGRESS CATALOG CARD NUMBER:
70-178479

PRINTED IN THE UNITED STATES OF AMERICA
BY
NEW WORLD BOOK MANUFACTURING CO., INC.
HALLANDALE, FLORIDA 33009

INFELICIA

BY

ADAH ISAACS MENKEN.

1868.
PHILADELPHIA.
NEW YORK.
BOSTON.

" Leaves pallid and sombre and ruddy,
Dead fruits of the fugitive years ;
Some stained as with wine and made bloody,
And some as with tears."

TO

CHARLES DICKENS.

CONTENTS.

PAGE

RESURGAM 9

DREAMS OF BEAUTY . . . . . · 14

MY HERITAGE 17

JUDITH 20

WORKING AND WAITING 24

THE RELEASE 27

IN VAIN 30

VENETIA 34

THE SHIP THAT WENT DOWN 36

BATTLE OF THE STARS 40

MYSELF 47

INTO THE DEPTHS 51

SALE OF SOULS 56

ONE YEAR AGO 61

GENIUS 63

DRIFTS THAT BAR MY DOOR 67

8   *CONTENTS.*

		PAGE
ASPIRATION	. . . .	72
MISERIMUS	. . . . . .	73
A MEMORY	. . . .	75
HEMLOCK IN THE FURROWS	. . . .	77
HEAR, O ISRAEL!	. . . . . .	82
WHERE THE FLOCKS SHALL BE LED	. .	87
PRO PATRIA	. . . .	90
"KARAZAH" TO "KARL"	. . . . .	97
A FRAGMENT	. . . . . .	98
THE AUTOGRAPH ON THE SOUL	. . .	103
ADELINA PATTI	. . . . . .	108
DYING	. . . .	109
SAVED	. . . .	115
ANSWER ME	. . . . . .	119
INFELIX	. . . .	124

INFELICIA.

RESURGAM.

I.

YES, yes, dear love! I am dead!
  Dead to you!
  Dead to the world!
  Dead for ever!
It was one young night in May.
The stars were strangled, and the moon was blind with the
  flying clouds of a black despair.
Years and years the songless soul waited to drift out
beyond the sea of pain where the shapeless life was
wrecked.
The red mouth closed down the breath that was hard
and fierce.
The mad pulse beat back the baffled life with a low
sob.
And so the stark and naked soul unfolded its wings to
the dimness of Death!
A lonely, unknown Death.
A Death that left this dumb, living body as his endless
mark.

9

And left these golden billows of hair to drown the whiteness of my bosom.

Left these crimson roses gleaming on my forehead to hide the dust of the grave.

And Death left an old light in my eyes, and old music for my tongue, to deceive the crawling worms that would seek my warm flesh.

But the purple wine that I quaff sends no thrill of Love and Song through my empty veins.

Yet my red lips are not pallid and horrified.

Thy kisses are doubtless sweet that throb out an eternal passion for me !

But I feel neither pleasure, passion nor pain.

So I am certainly dead.

Dead in this beauty !

Dead in this velvet and lace !

Dead in these jewels of light !

Dead in the music !

Dead in the dance !

II.

Why did I die ?

O love !   I waited—I waited years and years ago.

Once the blaze of a far-off edge of living Love crept up my horizon and promised a new moon of Poesy.

A soul's full life !

A soul's full love !

And promised that my voice should ring trancing shivers of rapt melody down the grooves of this dumb earth.

And promised that echoes should vibrate along the purple spheres of unfathomable seas, to the soundless folds of the clouds.

And promised that I should know the sweet sisterhood of the stars.

Promised that I should live with the crooked moon in her eternal beauty.

But a Midnight swooped down to bridegroom the Day.

The blazing Sphynx of that far off, echoless promise, shrank into a drowsy shroud that mocked the crying stars of my soul's unuttered song.

And so I died.

Died this uncoffined and unburied Death.

Died alone in the young May night.

Died with my fingers grasping the white throat of many a prayer.

III.

Yes, dear love, I died!

You smile because you see no cold, damp cerements of a lonely grave hiding the youth of my fair face.

No head-stone marks the gold of my poor unburied head.

But the flaunting poppy covered her red heart in the sand.

Who can hear the slow drip of blood from a dead soul?

No Christ of the Past writes on my laughing brow His "Resurgam."

Resurgam.

What is that when I have been dead these long weary years!

IV.

Silver walls of Sea!

Gold and spice laden barges!

White-sailed ships from Indian seas, with costly pearls and tropic wines go by unheeding!

None pause to lay one token at my feet.

No mariner lifts his silken banner for my answering hail.

No messages from the living to the dead.

Must all lips fall out of sound as the soul dies to be heard?

Shall Love send back no revelation through this interminable distance of Death?

Can He who promised the ripe Harvest forget the weeping Sower?

How can I stand here so calm?

I hear the clods closing down my coffin, and yet shriek not out like the pitiless wind, nor reach my wild arms after my dead soul!

Will no sun of fire again rise over the solemn East?

I am tired of the foolish moon showing only her haggard face above the rocks and chasms of my grave.

O Rocks! O Chasms! sink back to your black cradles in the West!

Leave me dead in the depths!

Leave me dead in the wine!

Leave me dead in the dance!

V.

How did I die?

The man I loved—he—he—ah, well!

There is no voice from the grave.

The ship that went down at sea, with seven times a thousand souls for Death, sent back no answer.

The breeze is voiceless that saw the sails shattered in the mad tempest, and heard the cry for mercy as one frail arm clung to the last spar of the sinking wreck.

Fainting souls rung out their unuttered messages to the silent clouds.

Alas! I died not so!

I died not so!

VI.

How did I die?

No man has wrenched his shroud from his stiffened corpse to say:

"*Ye murdered me!*"

No woman has died with enough of Christ in her soul to tear the bandage from her glassy eyes and say:

"*Ye crucified me!*"

Resurgam! Resurgam!

DREAMS OF BEAUTY.

VISIONS of Beauty, of Light, and of Love,
  Born in the soul of a Dream,
Lost, like the phantom-bird under the dove,
  When she flies over a stream—

Come ye through portals where angel wings droop,
  Moved by the heaven of sleep?
Or, are ye mockeries, crazing a soul,
  Doomed with its waking to weep?

I could believe ye were shadows of earth,
  Echoes of hopes that are vain,
But for the music ye bring to my heart,
  Waking its sunshine again.

And ye are fleeting. All vainly I strive
  Beauties like thine to portray;
Forth from my pencil the bright picture starts,
  And—ye have faded away.

Like to a bird that soars up from the spray,
  When we would fetter its wing;
Like to the song that spurns Memory's grasp
  When the voice yearneth to sing;

Like the cloud-glory that sunset lights up,
 When the storm bursts from its height;
Like the sheet-silver that rolls on the sea,
 When it is touched by the night—

Bright, evanescent, ye come and are gone,
 Visions of mystical birth;
Art that could paint you was never vouchsafed
 Unto the children of earth.

Yet in my soul there's a longing to tell
 All you have seemed unto me,
That unto others a glimpse of the skies
 You in their sorrow might be.

Vain is the wish. Better hope to describe
 All that the spirit desires,
When through a cloud of vague fancies and schemes
 Flash the Promethean fires.

Let me then think of ye, Visions of Light,
 Not as the tissue of dreams,
But as realities destined to be
 Bright in Futurity's beams.

Ideals formed by a standard of earth
 Sink at Reality's shrine
Into the human and weak like ourselves,
 Losing the essence divine;

But the fair pictures that fall from above
 On the heart's mirror sublime

Carry a signature written in tints,
　　Bright with the future of time.

And the heart, catching them, yieldeth a spark
　　Under each stroke of the rod—
Sparks that fly upward and light the New Life,
　　Burning an incense to God !

MY HERITAGE.

" MY heritage !" It is to live within
    The marts of Pleasure and of Gain, yet be
No willing worshiper at either shrine ;
To think, and speak, and act, not for my pleasure,
But others'. The veriest slave of time
And circumstances. Fortune's toy !
To hear of fraud, injustice, and oppression,
And feel who is the unshielded victim.
        Cold friends and causeless foes !
        Proud thoughts that rise to fall.
Bright stars that set in seas of blood ;
Affections, which are passions, lava-like
Destroying what they rest upon.   Love's
Fond and fervid tide preparing icebergs
That fragile bark, this loving human heart.
        O'ermastering Pride !
        Ruler of the Soul !
Life, with all its changes, cannot bow ye.
        Soul-subduing Poverty !
That lays his iron, cold grasp upon the high
Free spirit : strength, sorrow-born, that bends
But breaks not in his clasp—all, all
These are "my heritage !"
And mine to know a reckless human love, all passion

2   17

and intensity, and see a mist come o'er the scene, a dim-
ness steal o'er the soul !

Mine to dream of joy and wake to wretchedness !
Mine to stand on the brink of life
One little moment where the fresh'ning breeze
Steals o'er the languid lip and brow, telling
Of forest leaf, and ocean wave, and happy
Homes, and cheerful toil ; and bringing gently
To this wearied heart its long-forgotten
Dreams of gladness.

But turning the fevered cheek to meet the soft kiss of
the winds, my eyes look to the sky, where I send up my
soul in thanks.   The sky is clouded—no stars—no music
—the heavens are hushed.

My poor soul comes back to me, weary and disap-
pointed.

The very breath of heaven, that comes to all, comes not
to me.

Bound in iron gyves of unremitting toil, my vital air is
wretchedness—what need I any other ?

"My heritage !"   The shrouded eye, the trampled leaf,
wind-driven and soiled with dust—these tell the tale.

Mine to watch
The glorious light of intellect
Burn dimly, and expire ; and mark the soul,
Though born in Heaven, pause in its high career,
Wave in its course, and fall to grovel in
The darkness of earth's contamination, till
Even Death shall scorn to give a thing
So low his welcome greeting !
Who would be that pale,

Blue mist, that hangs so low in air, like Hope
That has abandoned earth, yet reacheth
Not the stars in their proud homes?
A dying eagle, striving to reach the sun?
A little child talking to the gay clouds as they flaunt
past in their purple and crimson robes?
A timid little flower singing to the grand old trees?
Foolish waves, leaping up and trying to kiss the moon?
A little bird mocking the stars?
Yet this is what men call Genius.

JUDITH.

"Repent, or I will come unto thee quickly, and will fight thee with the sword of my mouth."—REVELATION ii. 16.

I.

ASHKELON is not cut off with the remnant of a valley.
Baldness dwells not upon Gaza.
The field of the valley is mine, and it is clothed in verdure.
The steepness of Baal-perazim is mine;
And the Philistines spread themselves in the valley of Rephaim.
They shall yet be delivered into my hands.
For the God of Battles has gone before me!
The sword of the mouth shall smite them to dust.
I have slept in the darkness—
But the seventh angel woke me, and giving me a sword of flame, points to the blood-ribbed cloud, that lifts his reeking head above the mountain.
Thus am I the prophet.
I see the dawn that heralds to my waiting soul the advent of power.
Power that will unseal the thunders!
Power that will give voice to graves!

20

Graves of the living;
Graves of the dying;
Graves of the sinning;
Graves of the loving;
Graves of despairing;
And oh! graves of the deserted!
These shall speak, each as their voices shall be loosed.
And the day is dawning.

II.

Stand back, ye Philistines!
Practice what ye preach to me;
I heed ye not, for I know ye all.
Ye are living burning lies, and profanation to the garments which with stately steps ye sweep your marble palaces.
Your palaces of Sin, around which the damning evidence of guilt hangs like a reeking vapor.
Stand back!
I would pass up the golden road of the world.
A place in the ranks awaits me.
I know that ye are hedged on the borders of my path.
Lie and tremble, for ye well know that I hold with iron grasp the battle axe.
Creep back to your dark tents in the valley.
Slouch back to your haunts of crime.
Ye do not know me, neither do ye see me.
But the sword of the mouth is unsealed, and ye coil yourselves in slime and bitterness at my feet.
I mix your jeweled heads, and your gleaming eyes, and your hissing tongues with the dust.

My garments shall bear no mark of ye.

When I shall return this sword to the angel, your foul blood will not stain its edge.

It will glimmer with the light of truth, and the strong arm shall rest.

III.

Stand back!

I am no Magdalene waiting to kiss the hem of your garment.

It is mid-day.

See ye not what is written on my forehead?

I am Judith!

I wait for the head of my Holofernes!

Ere the last tremble of the conscious death-agony shall have shuddered, I will show it to ye with the long black hair clinging to the glazed eyes, and the great mouth opened in search of voice, and the strong throat all hot and reeking with blood, that will thrill me with wild unspeakable joy as it courses down my bare body and dabbles my cold feet!

My sensuous soul will quake with the burden of so much bliss.

Oh, what wild passionate kisses will I draw up from that bleeding mouth!

I will strangle this pallid throat of mine on the sweet blood!

I will revel in my passion.

At midnight I will feast on it in the darkness.

For it was that which thrilled its crimson tides of reckless passion through the blue veins of my life, and made them leap up in the wild sweetness of Love and agony of Revenge !

I am starving for this feast.

Oh forget not that I am Judith !

And I know where sleeps Holofernes.

WORKING AND WAITING.

Suggested by Carl Müller's Cast of the Seamstress, at the Dusseldorf
Gallery.

I.

LOOK on that form, once fit for the sculptor!
 Look on that cheek, where the roses have died!
Working and waiting have robbed from the artist
 All that his marble could show for its pride.
  Statue-like sitting
  Alone, in the flitting
And wind-haunted shadows that people her hearth.
  God protect all of us—
  God shelter all of us
From the reproach of such scenes upon earth!

II.

All the day long, and through the cold midnight,
 Still the hot needle she wearily plies.
Haggard and white as the ghost of a Spurned One,
 Sewing white robes for the Chosen One's eyes—
  Lost in her sorrow,
  But for the morrow
Phantom-like speaking in every stitch—
  God protect all of us—
  God shelter all of us
From the Curse, born with each sigh for the Rich!
24

III.

Low burns the lamp. Fly swifter, thou needle—
  Swifter, thou asp for the breast of the poor!
Else the pale light will be stolen by Pity,
  Ere of the vital part thou hast made sure.
      Dying, yet living:
      All the world's giving
Barely the life that runs out with her thread.
      God protect all of us—
      God shelter all of us
From her last glance, as she follows the Dead!

IV.

What if the morning finds her still bearing
  All the soul's load of a merciless lot!
Fate will not lighten a grain of the burden
  While the poor bearer by man is forgot.
      Sewing and sighing!
      Sewing and dying!
What to such life is a day or two more?
      God protect all of us—
      God shelter all of us
From the new day's lease of woe to the Poor!

V.

Hasten, ye winds! and yield her the mercy
  Lying in sleep on your purified breath;
Yield her the mercy, enfolding a blessing,
  Yield her the mercy whose signet is Death.

In her toil stopping,
See her work dropping—
Fate, thou art merciful !   Life, thou art done !
God protect all of us—
God shelter all of us
From the heart breaking, and yet living on !

VI.

Winds that have sainted her, tell ye the story
Of the young life by the needle that bled ;
Making its bridge over Death's soundless waters
Out of a swaying and soul-cutting thread.
Over it going,
All the world knowing !
Thousands have trod it, foot-bleeding, before !
God protect all of us—
God shelter all of us,
Should she look back from the Opposite Shore !

THE RELEASE.

I.

"Carry me out of the host, for I am wounded."

THE battle waged strong.
    A fainting soul was borne from the host.
The tears robed themselves in the scarlet of guilt, and
    crowned with iron of wrong, they trod heavily on the
    wounded soul,
Bound close to the dark prison-walls, with the clanking
    chains of old Error.
Malice and Envy crept up the slimy sides of the turrets to
    mark out with gore-stained fingers the slow hours of
    the night.
The remorseless Past stood ever near, breathing through
    the broken chords of life its never-ending dirge.
Yet, Ahab-like, the poor soul lingered on, bleeding and
    pining, pleading and praying.
Only through its mournful windows did the yearning soul
    dare speak ;
Still through the tears did it ever vainly reach outward
    some kindred soul to seek.
Unheeding did the ranks sweep by ;
And the weary soul sank back with all its deep unuttered
    longings to the loneliness of its voiceless world.

Hearing only the measured tread of Guile and Deceit on
their sentinel round.

Wherefore was that poor soul of all the host so wounded?
It struggled bravely.

Wherefore was it doomed and prisoned to pine and strive
apart?

It battled to the last.   Can it be that this captive soul was
a changeling, and battled and struggled in a body not its
own?

Must Error ever bind the fetters deep into the shrinking
flesh?

Will there come no angel to loose them?

And will Truth lift up her lamp at the waking?

Shall the cold tomb of the body grow warm and voice
forth all the speechless thought of the soul when the
sleeping dead shall rise?

Will there be no uprising in this world?

O! impatient Soul, wait, wait, wait.

II.

> "The Angel
> Who driveth away the demon band
> Bids the din of battle cease."

O prisoned Soul, up in your turrets so high, look down
from thy windows to-day!

Dash down the rusty chains of old Error, and unbar the
iron doors,

Break the bonds of the Past on the anvil of the Present.

O give me some token for the music that I have sent
through your lonely chambers!

Wave but the tip of your white wing in greeting to the
Angel that I have sent you !

Look forth on thy fellow Soul pausing at the gate !

List to the sound of his voice that rushes past the red
roof, and with unfurled wings, sweeps up its music
through the ivory gates to thee !

No other song can thrill its echoes up to thy captive life.

For this Angel hath chilled the hot hand of Sin, and
crushed down the grave of the crimson eyes of the
Past.

The daylight looms up softly, and feathery Hope is on
guard.

O waiting Soul, come forth from your turrets, so lone and
high !

Listen to the low sweet music of promise, rushing wildly
through floods of God-inspiration of love, up to Eter-
nity.

Tremble not at the bars.   Come forth !

The tongue you fear sleeps in frozen silence, and doth thy
mighty secret keep.

IN VAIN.

I.

O FOOLISH tears, go back !
     Learn to cover your jealous pride far down in the nerveless heart that ye are voices for.

Your sobbings mar the unfinished picture that my trembling life would fill up to greet its dawn.

I know, poor heart, that you are reaching up to a Love that finds not all its demands in thy weak pulse.

And I know that you sob up your red tears to my face, because—because—*others* who care less for his dear Love may, each day, open their glad eyes his lightest wish to bless.

But, jealous heart, *we* will not give him from drops that overflow thy rim.

We will fathom the mysteries of earth, of air and of sea, to fill thy broad life with beauty, and then empty all its very depths of light deep into his wide soul !

II.

Ah ! When I am a cloud—a pliant, floating cloud—I will haunt the Sun-God for some eternal ray of Beauty.

I will wind my soft arms around the wheels of his blazing chariot, till he robes me in gorgeous trains of gold !

I will sing to the stars till they crown me with their richest jewels!

I will plead to the angels for the whitest, broadest wings that ever walled their glorious heights around a dying soul!

Then I will flaunt my light down the steep grooves of space into this dark, old world, until Eyes of Love will brighten for me!

III.

When I am a flower—a wild, sweet flower—I will open my glad blue eyes to one alone.

I will bloom in his footsteps, and muffle their echoes with my velvet lips.

So near him will I grow that 'his breath shall mark kisses on all my green leaves!

I will fill his deep soul with all the eternal fragrance of my love!

Yes, I will be a violet—a wild sweet violet—and sigh my very life away for him!

IV.

When I am a bird—a white-throated bird—all trimmed in plumage of crimson and gold, I will sing to one alone.

I will come from the sea—the broad blue sea—and fold my wings with olive-leaves to the glad tidings of his hopes!

I will come from the forest—the far old forest—where sighs and tears of reckless loves have never moaned away the morning of poor lives.

I will come from the sky, with songs of an angel, and flutter into his soul to see how I may be all melody to him !

Yes, I will be a bird—a loving, docile bird—and furl my wild wings, and shut my sad eyes in his breast !

V.

When I am a wave—a soft, white wave—I will run up from ocean's purple spheres, and murmur out my low sweet voice to one alone.

I will dash down to the cavern of gems and lift up to his eyes Beauty that will drink light from the Sun !

I will bring blue banners that angels have lost from the clouds.

Yes, I will be a wave—a happy, dancing wave—and leap up in the sunshine to lay my crown of spray-pearls at his feet.

VI.

Alas ! poor heart, what am I now ?

A weed—a frail, bitter weed—growing outside the garden wall.

All day straining my dull eyes to see the blossoms within, as they wave their crimson flags to the wind.

And yet my dark leaves pray to be as glorious as the rose.

My bitter stalks would be as sweet as the violet if they could.

I try to bloom up into the light.

My poor, yearning soul to Heaven would open its velvet eyes of fire.

Oh ! the love of Beauty through every fibre of my lonely life is trembling !

Every floating cloud and flying bird draws up jealous Envy an.l bleeding Love !

So passionately wild in me is this burning unspeakable thirst to grow all beauty, all grace, all melody to one—and to him alone !

3

VENETIA.

BRIGHT as the light that burns at night,
   In the starry depths of Aiden,
When star and moon in leafy June
   With love and joy are laden ;
Bright as the light from moon and star,
   Stars in glorious cluster,
Be the lights that shine on this life of thine,
   Be the beauty of its lustre.

Beneath the moon in leafy June,
   Sweet vows are fondly spoken ;
Beneath the stars, the silvery tune
   Of music floats unbroken.
Beneath the sky, and moon and stars,
   Come nestling birds of beauty,
And Love with Bliss, and Hope with Joy
   Troop down the path of duty.

Oh ! ever may'st thou, bird of mine,
   Nestle to my bosom sweetly,
Birds of my soaring, feathery hope,
   That flyeth to me so fleetly.
Oh ! ever thus may vows of love
   My yearning soul inherit—
Vows unbroken, as those spoken
   By celestial spirit.

And when the vow thou breathest now,
  For me, for mine and only,
Shall float to Aiden's starry land,
  Where none are lost or lonely,
Believe me, when the angel bends
  His loving ear to listen,
Radiant will be the smile that blends
  With the beauteous tears that glisten.

For darling, those who love us here
  With tender, sweet emotion,
With love that knows no stop or fear,
  But burneth with devotion ;
'Tis only but another proof
  That something good is left us,
That we are not by Heaven forgot,
  That Heaven hath not bereft us.

THE SHIP THAT WENT DOWN.

I.

WHO hath not sent out ships to sea?
    Who hath not toiled through light and dark ness to
    make them strong for battle?
And how we freighted them with dust from the mountain
    mines!
And red gold, coined from the heart's blood, rich in
    Youth, Love and Beauty!
And we have fondly sent forth on their white decks seven
    times a hundred souls.
Sent them out like sea-girt worlds full of hope, love, care,
    and faith.
O mariners, mariners, watch and beware!

II.

See the Ship that I sent forth!
How proudly she nods her regal head to each saluting
    wave!
How defiantly she flaps her white sails at the sun, who, in
    envy of her beauty, screens his face behind a passing
    cloud, yet never losing sight of her.
The ocean hath deck'd himself in robes of softest blue,
    and lifted his spray-flags to greet her.

36

The crimson sky hath swooped down from her Heaven-
　Palace, and sitteth with her white feet dabbling in the
　borders of the sea, while she sendeth sweet promises
　on the wings of the wind to my fair Ship.
O mariners, mariners, why did ye not watch and beware?

III.

The faithless sky is black.
The ocean howls on the Ship's rough track.
The strong wind, and the shouting rain swept by like an
　armed host whooping out their wild battle-cry.
The tall masts dip their heads down into the deep.
The wet shrouds rattle as they seem to whisper prayers to
　themselves ;
But the waves leap over their pallid sails, and grapple and
　gnaw at their seams.
The poor Ship shrieks and groans out her despair.
She rises up to plead with the sky, and sinks down the
　deep valley of water to pray.
O God, make us strong for the battle!

IV.

What says the mariner so hurried and pale?
No need to whisper it, speak out, speak!
Danger and peril you say?
Does your quivering lip and white cheek mean that the
　good Ship must go down?
Why stand ye idle and silent?
O sailors, rouse your brave hearts!
Man the rocking masts, and reef the rattling sails!

Heed not the storm-fires that so terribly burn in the black
    sky !
Heed not the storm-mad sea below !
Heed not the death-cry of the waves !
Foot to foot, hand to hand !   Toil on brave hearts !
        Our good Ship must be saved !
        Before us lies the goal !

V.

Too late, too late !
The life-boats are lost.
The rent spars have groaned out their lives, and the white
    sails have shrouded them in their rough beds of
    Death.
Strong mariners have fainted and failed in the terror and
    strife.
White lips are grasping for breath, and trembling out
    prayers, and waiting to die.
And the Ship, once so fair, lies a life-freighted wreck.
The Promises, Hopes, and Loves, are sinking, sinking
    away.
The winds shriek out their joy, and the waves shout out
    their anthem of Death.
        Pitiless wind !
        Pitiless ocean !

VI.

O mariners, is there no help ?
Is there no beacon-light in the distance ?

Dash the tears of blood from your eyes, and look over
    these Alps of water !
See ye no sail glittering through the darkness?
Is there no help ?
Must they all die, all die ?
So much of Youth, so much of Beauty, so much of Life ?
The waves answer with ravenous roar ;
They grapple like demons the trembling Ship !
Compassless, rudderless, the poor Ship pleads.
In vain ! in vain !
With a struggling, shivering, dying grasp, my good Ship
    sank down, down, down to the soundless folds of the
    fathomless ocean.
            Lost—lost—lost.

BATTLE OF THE STARS.

(*After Ossian.*)

A LONE on the hill of storms
    The voice of the wind shrieks through the moun-
    tain.
The torrent rushes down the rocks.
Red are hundred streams of the light-covered paths of the
    dead.
Shield me in from the storm,
I that am a daughter of the stars, and wear the purple and
    gold of bards, with the badges of Love on my white
    bosom.
I heed not the battle-cry of souls !
I that am chained on this Ossa of existence.
Sorrow hath bound her frozen chain about the wheels of
    my chariot of fire wherein my soul was wont to ride.
Stars, throw off your dark robes, and lead me to the palace
    where my Eros rests on his iron shield of war, his
    gleaming sword in the scabbard, his hounds haunting
    around him.
The water and the storm cry aloud.
I hear not the voice of my Love.
Why delays the chief of the stars his promise ?
Here is the terrible cloud, and here the cloud of life with
    its many-colored sides.

40

Thou didst promise to be with me when night should trail
 her dusky skirts along the borders of my soul.
O wind! O thought! Stream and torrent, be ye silent!
Let the wanderer hear my voice.
Eros, I am waiting. Why delay thy coming? It is Atha
 calls thee.
See the calm moon comes forth.
The flood is silver in the vale.
The rocks are gray on the steep.
I see him not on the mountain brow;
The hounds come not with the glad tidings of his ap-
 proach.
I wait for morning in my tears.
Rear the tomb, but close it not till Eros comes:
Not unharmed will return the eagle from the field of foes.
But Atha will not mark thy wounds, she will be silent in
 her blood.
Love, the great Dreamer, will listen to her voice, and she
 will sleep on the soft bosom of the hills.
O Love! thou Mighty Leveler,
Thou alone canst lay the shepherd's crook beside the
 sceptre,
Thou art the King of the Stars.
Music floats up to thee, receives thy breath, thy burning
 kisses, and comes back with messages to children of
 earth.
Thou art pitiful and bountiful.
Although housed with the golden-haired Son of the Sky,
 with stars for thy children, dwelling in the warm
 clouds, and sleeping on the silver shields of War, yet
 ye do not disdain the lonely Atha that hovers round

the horizon of your Grand Home. You awake and
come forth arrayed in trailing robes of glory, with
blessing and with song to greet her that seeketh thy
mighty presence.

Thy hand giveth Morn her power;
Thy hand lifteth the mist from the hills;
Thy hand createth all of Beauty;
Thy hand giveth Morn her rosy robes;
Thy hands bound up the wounds of Eros after the battle:
Thy hands lifted him to the skirts of the wind, like the
    eagle of the forest.
Thy hands have bound his brow with the spoils of the
    foe.
Thy hands have given to me the glittering spear, and hel-
    met of power and might;
Nor settles the darkness on me.
The fields of Heaven are mine.
I will hush the sullen roar of the enemy.
Warriors shall lift their shields to me.
My arm is strong, my sword defends the weak.
I will loose the thong of the Oppressed, and dash to hell
    the Oppressor.
A thousand warriors stretch their spears around me.
I battle for the stars.
It was thy hands, O Love, that loosed my golden tresses,
    and girded my white limbs in armor, and made me
    leader of the armies of Heaven.
Thy voice aroused the sluggard soul.
Thy voice calleth back the sleeping dead.
Thou alone, O Mighty Ruler, canst annihilate space, hush
    the shrieking wind, hide the white-haired waves,

and bear me to the arms and burning kisses of my Eros.

And it is thou who makest beautiful the prison-houses of earth.

I once was chained to their darkness, but thou, O Love, brought crimson roses to lay on my pale bosom, and covered the cold damp walls with the golden shields of the sun, and left thy purple garments whereon my weary bleeding feet might rest.

And when black-winged night rolled along the sky, thy shield covered the moon, and thy hands threw back the prison-roof, and unfolded the gates of the clouds, and I slept in the white arms of the stars.

And thou, O Beam of Life! didst thou not forget the lonely prisoner of Chillon in his gloomy vault? thy blessed ray of Heaven-light stole in and made glad his dreams.

Thou hast lifted the deep-gathered mist from the dungeons of Spielberg ;

Ugolino heard thy voice in his hopeless cell :

Thy blessed hand soothed Damiens on his bed of steel ;

It is thy powerful hand that lights up to Heaven the inspired life of Garabaldi.

And it is thy undying power that will clothe Italy in the folds of thy wings, and rend the helmet from the dark brow of old Austria, and bury her in the eternal tomb of darkness.

Thou didst not forget children of earth, who roll the waves of their souls to our ship of the sky.

But men are leagued against us—strong mailed men of earth,

Around the dwellers in the clouds they rise in wrath.

No words come forth, they seize their blood-stained daggers.

Each takes his hill by night, at intervals they darkly stand counting the power and host of Heaven.

Their black unmuzzled hounds howl their impatience as we come on watch in our glittering armor.

The hills no longer smile up to greet us, they are covered with these tribes of earth leading their war-dogs, and leaving their footprints of blood.

Unequal bursts the hum of voices, and the clang of arms between the roaring wind.

And they dare to blaspheme the very stars, and even God on His high throne in the Heaven of Heavens, by pleading for Love.

Love sacrifices all things to bless the thing it loves, not destroy.

Go back to your scorching homes ;

Go back to your frozen souls ;

Go back to your seas of blood ;

Go back to your chains, your loathsome charnel houses ;

Give us the green bosom of the hills to rest upon ;

Broad over them rose the moon.

O Love, Great Ruler, call upon thy children to buckle on the armor of war, for behold the enemy blackens all earth in waiting for us.

See the glittering of their unsheathed swords.

They bear blood-stained banners of death and destruction.

And, lo, their Leader comes forth on the Pale Horse.

His sword is a green meteor half-extinguished.

His face is without form, and dark withal, dark as the tales
    of other times, before the light of song arose.
Mothers, clasp your new-born children close to your white
    bosoms !
Daughters of the stars, sleep no more, the enemy ap-
    proacheth !
Look to your white shields !
Bind up your golden tresses !
See the blood upon the pale breasts of your sisters.
Where are your banners ?
O sluggards, awake to the call of the Mighty Ruler !
Hear ye not the clash of arms ?   Arise around me, chil-
    dren of the Land Unknown.
Up, up, grasp your helmet and your spear !
Let each one look upon her shield as the ruler of War.
Come forth in your purple robes, sound your silver-tongue
    trumpets ;
Rush upon the enemy with your thousand and thousands
    of burnished spears !
Let your voices ring through the Universe, " Liberty,
    liberty for the stars."   Thunder it on the ears of the
    guilty and the doomed !
Sound it with the crash of Heaven's wrath to the hearts
    of branded—God-cursed things who have stood up
    and scorned their Maker with laughing curses, as
    they dashed the crown from her brow, and hurled her
    into Hell.
Pray ye not for them, hills !   Heed ye not, O winds, their
    penitence is feigned !
Let your voices, O floods, be hushed ! stars, close your
    mighty flanks, and battle on them !

Chain them down close to the fire!

They were merciless, bind their blood-stained hands.

They are fiends, and if ye loose them they will tear children from their mothers, wives from their husbands, sisters from their brothers, daughters from their fathers.

And these fiends, these children of eternal damnation, these men will tear souls from bodies, and then smear their hands with blood, and laugh as they sprinkle it in the dead up-turned faces of their victims.

It is Atha thy leader that calls to you.

Beat them down, beat them down.

I know these war-dogs.

They strangled my warrior, Eros!

Warrior of my soul;

Warrior of the strong race of Eagles!

His crimson life crushed out on the white sails of a ship.

Battle them down to dust.

Battle them back into their own slimy souls;

Battle them, ye starry armies of Heaven, down into the silent sea of their own blood;

Battle on, the wind is with ye;

Battle on, the sun is with ye;

Battle on, the waves are with ye;

The Angels are with ye;

God is with us!

MYSELF.

" La patience est amère ; mais le fruit en est doux !"

I.

A WAY down into the shadowy depths of the Real I once lived.

I thought that to seem was to be.

But the waters of Marah were beautiful, yet they were bitter.

I waited, and hoped, and prayed ;

Counting the heart-throbs and the tears that answered them.

Through my earnest pleadings for the True, I learned that the mildest mercy of life was a smiling sneer ;

And that the business of the world was to lash with vengeance all who dared to be what their God had made them.

Smother back tears to the red blood of the heart !

Crush out things called souls !

No room for them here !

II.

Now I gloss my pale face with laughter, and sail my voice on with the tide.

Decked in jewels and lace, I laugh beneath the gas-light's glare, and quaff the purple wine.

But the minor-keyed soul is standing naked and hungry upon one of Heaven's high hills of light.

Standing and waiting for the blood of the feast!

Starving for one poor word!

Waiting for God to launch out some beacon on the boundless shores of this Night.

Shivering for the uprising of some soft wing under which it may creep, lizard-like, to warmth and rest.

Waiting!   Starving and shivering!

III.

Still I trim my white bosom with crimson roses ; for none shall see the thorns.

I bind my aching brow with a jeweled crown, that none shall see the iron one beneath.

My silver-sandaled feet keep impatient time to the music, because I cannot be calm.

I laugh at earth's passion-fever of Love ; yet I know that God is near to the soul on the hill, and hears the ceaseless ebb and flow of a hopeless love, through all my laughter.

But if I can cheat my heart with the old comfort, that love can be forgotten, is it not better?

After all, living is but to play a part!

The poorest worm would be a jewel-headed snake if she could!

IV.

All this grandeur of glare and glitter has its night-time.

The pallid eyelids must shut out smiles and daylight.

Then I fold my cold hands, and look down at the restless rivers of a love that rushes through my life.

Unseen and unknown they tide on over black rocks and chasms of Death.

Oh, for one sweet word to bridge their terrible depths !

O jealous soul ! why wilt thou crave and yearn for what thou canst not have ?

And life is so long—so long.

V.

With the daylight comes the business of living.

The prayers that I sent trembling up the golden thread of hope all come back to me.

I lock them close in my bosom, far under the velvet and roses of the world.

For I know that stronger than these torrents of passion is the soul that hath lifted itself up to the hill.

What care I for his careless laugh ?

I do not sigh ; but I know that God hears the life-blood dripping as I, too, laugh.

I would not be thought a foolish rose, that flaunts her red heart out to the sun.

Loving is not living !

VI.

Yet through all this I know that night will roll back

4

from the still, gray plain of heaven, and that my triumph shall rise sweet with the dawn!

When these mortal mists shall unclothe the world, then shall I be known as I am!

When I dare be dead and buried behind a wall of wings, then shall he know me!

When this world shall fall, like some old ghost, wrapped in the black skirts of the wind, down into the fathomless eternity of fire, then shall souls uprise!

When God shall lift the frozen seal from struggling voices, then shall we speak!

When the purple-and-gold of our inner natures shall be lighted up in the Eternity of Truth, then will love be mine!

I can wait.

INTO THE DEPTHS.

I.

LOST—lost—lost!
    To me, for ever, the seat near the blood of the feast.

To me, for ever, the station near the Throne of Love!

To me, for ever, the Kingdom of Heaven—and I the least.

> Oh, the least in love—
> The least in joy—
> The least in life—
> The least in death—
> The least in beauty—
> The least in eternity.

So much of rich, foaming, bubbling human blood drank down into the everlasting sea of Sin.

The jasper gates are closed on the crimson highway of the clouds.

> The Seven Angels stand on guard.
> Seven thunders utter their voices.

And the angels have not sealed up those things which the seven thunders have uttered.

I have pleaded to the seventh angel for the little book.

But he heedeth me not.

All life is bitter, not one drop as sweet as honey.

And yet I prophesy before many people, and nations, and tongues, and kings !

II.

Lost—lost—lost !

The little golden key which the first angel entrusted to me.

The gates are closed, and I may not enter.

Yet arrayed in folds of white, these angels are more terrible to me than the fabled watcher of the Hesperides golden treasures.

Because it is I alone of all God's creatures that am shut out.

For others the bolts are withdrawn, and the little book unsealed.

With wistful eyes, and longing heart, I wander in the distance, waiting for the angels to sleep.

Tremblingly I peer through the gloaming of horrid shadows, and visions of wasted moments.

But the white eyelids of the angels never droop.

In vain I plead to them that it was I who built the throne.

In vain do I tell them that it was I who gemmed it with Faith and Truth, and the dews of my life's morn.

In vain do I tell them that they are my hopes which they stand in solemn guard to watch.

In vain do I plead my right as queen of the starry highway.

In vain do I bind my golden tresses with the pale lilies of the valley.

In vain do I display to them my purple broidered robes, and the silver badge of God's eternal bards that I wear on my white bosom.

In vain do I wind my soft arms around their silver-sandaled feet.

They heed me not.

But point to the whirlpool called the world.

Must the warm, living, loving soul a wanderer be?

Are all its yearnings vain?

Are all its prayings vain?

Will there be no light to guide me?

Will there be strong arm at the helm?

Must the full lamp of life wane so early?

Ah, I see, all is lost—lost—lost!

III.

Deep into the depths!

Struggling all the day-time—weeping all the night-time!

Writing away all vitality.

Talking to people, nations, tongues, and kings that heed me not.

Cast out of my own kingdom on to the barren battle-plain of bloodless life.

A thousand foes advancing?

A thousand weapons glancing!

And I in the sternest scene of strife.

Panting wildly in the race.

Malice and Envy on the track.

Fleet of foot, they front me with their daggers at my breast.

All heedless of my tears and prayers, they tear the white flowers from my brow, and the olive leaves from my breast, and soil with their blood-marked hands the broidered robes of purple beauty.

Life's gems are torn from me, and in scattered fragments around me lie.

All lost—lost—lost!

IV.

Out of the depths have I cried unto thee, O Lord!
Weeping all the night-time.
Weeping sad and chill through the lone woods.
Straying 'mong the ghostly trees.
Wandering through the rustling leaves.
Sobbing to the moon, whose icy light wraps me like a shroud.

Leaning on a hoary rock, praying to the mocking stars.

With Love's o'erwhelming power startling my soul like an earthquake shock.

I lift my voice above the low howl of the winds to call my Eros to come and give me light and life once more.

His broad arms can raise me up to the light, and his red lips can kiss me back to life.

I heed not the storm of the world, nor the clashing of its steel.

I wait—wait—wait!

V.

How can I live so deep into the depths with all this wealth of love?

Oh, unspeakable, passionate fire of love !
      Cold blood heedeth ye not.
      Cold eyes know ye not.
But in this wild soul of seething passion we have warmed together.
I feel thy lava tide dashing recklessly through every blue course !
Grand, beauteous Love !
Let us live alone, far from the world of battle and pain, where we can forget this grief that has plunged me into the depths.
We will revel in ourselves.
Come, Eros, thou creator of this divine passion, come and lay my weary head on your bosom.
Draw me close up to your white breast and lull me to sleep.
Smooth back the damp, tangled mass from my pale brow.
      I am so weary of battle—
      Take this heavy shield.
      I am so weary of toil—
      Loosen my garments.
Now, wrap me close in your bosom to rest.
Closer—closer still !
Let your breath warm my cold face.
This is life—this is love !
Oh, kiss me till I sleep—till I sleep—I sleep.

SALE OF SOULS.

I.

OH, I am wild—wild!
　　Angels of the weary-hearted, come to thy child.
Spread your white wings over me!
　　　　　Tenderly, tenderly,
　　　　　Lovingly, lovingly,
　　　　　Plead for me, plead for me!

II.

Souls for sale! souls for sale!
Souls for gold! who'll buy?
In the pent-up city, through the wild rush and beat of
　　human hearts, I hear this unceasing, haunting cry:
　　　　　Souls for sale! souls for sale!
　　　　　Through mist and gloom,
　　　　　Through hate and love,
　　　　　Through peace and strife,
　　　　　Through wrong and right,
　　　　　Through life and death,
The hoarse voice of the world echoes up the cold gray
　　sullen river of life.
　　　　　On, on, on!

No silence until it shall have reached the solemn sea of
    God's for ever ;
            No rest, no sleep ;
Waking through the thick gloom of midnight, to hear the
    damning cry as it mingles and clashes with the rough
    clang of gold.
            Poor Heart, poor Heart,
            Alas ! I know thy fears.

III.

The hollow echoes that the iron-shod feet of the years
    throw back on the sea of change still vibrate through
    the grave-yard of prayers and tears ;—
            Prayers that fell unanswered,
            Tears that followed hopelessly.
But pale Memory comes back through woe and shame
    and strife, bearing on her dark wings their buried
    voices ;
Like frail helpless barks, they wail through the black sea
    of the crowded city,
            Mournfully, mournfully.

IV.

Poor Heart, what do the waves say to thee ?
The sunshine laughed on the hill sides.
The link of years that wore a golden look bound me to
    woman-life by the sweet love of my Eros, and the
    voice of one who made music to call me mother.
Weak Heart, weak Heart !

Oh, now I reel madly on through clouds and storms and
     night.
The hills have grown dark,
They lack the grace of my golden-haired child, to climb
     their steep sides, and bear me their smiles in the
     blue-eyed violets of our spring-time.
Sad Heart, what do the hills say to thee?
They speak of my Eros, and how happily in the dim dis-
     colored hours we dreamed away the glad light, and
     watched the gray robes of night as she came through
     the valley, and ascended on her way to the clouds.
          Kisses of joy, and kisses of life,
          Kisses of heaven, and kisses of earth,
Clinging and clasping white hands;
Mingling of soft tresses;
Murmurings of love, and murmurings of life,
With the warm blood leaping up in joy to answer its
     music;
The broad shelter of arms wherein dwelt peace and con-
     tent, so sweet to love.
All, all were mine.
          Loving Heart, loving Heart,
Hush the wailing and sobbing voice of the past;
Sleep in thy rivers of the soul,
          Poor Heart.

V.

          Souls for sale!
The wild cry awoke the god of ambition, that slumbered
     in the bosom of Eros;

From out the tents he brought forth his-shield and spear,
　　to see them smile back at the sun ;
Clad in armor, he went forth to the cities of the world,
　　where brave men battle for glory, and souls are bar-
　　tered for gold.
Weeping and fearing, haggard and barefoot, I clung to him
　　with my fainting child.
Weary miles of land and water lay in their waste around
　　us.
We reached the sea of the city.
Marble towers lifted their proud heads beyond the scope
　　of vision.
Wild music mingled with laughter.
The tramp of hoofs on the iron streets, and the cries of the
　　drowning, and the curses of the damned were all heard
　　in that Babel, where the souls of men can be bought
　　for gold.
All the air seemed dark with evil wings.
And all that was unholy threw their shadows everywhere,
　　　　Shadows on the good,
　　　　Shadows on the bad,
　　　　Shadows on the lowly,
　　　　Shadows on the lost !
All tossing upon the tide of rushing, restless destiny ;
Upon all things written :
　　　　Souls for sale !
　　　　Lost Heart, lost Heart !

VI.

A soul mantled in glory, and sold to the world ;

O horrible sale !
O seal of blood !
Give back my Eros.
His bowstring still sounds on the blast, yet his arrow was broken in the fall.
Oh leave me not on the wreck of this dark-bosomed ship while Eros lies pale on the rocks of the world.
Driven before the furious gale by the surging ocean's strife ;
The strong wind lifting up the sounding sail, and whistling through the ropes and masts ; waves lash the many-colored sides of the ship, dash her against the oozy rocks.
The strength of old ocean roars.
The low booming of the signal gun is heard above the tempest.
Oh how many years must roll their slow length along my life, ere the land be in sight !
When will the morning dawn ?
When will the clouds be light ?
When will the storm be hushed ?
It is so dark and cold.
Angels of the weary-hearted, come to your child !
Build your white wings around me.
          Tenderly, tenderly,
          Pity me, pity me.

ONE YEAR AGO.

IN feeling I was but a child,
  When first we met—one year ago,
As free and guileless as the bird,
  That roams the dreary woodland through.

My heart was all a pleasant world
  Of sunbeams dewed with April tears :
Life's brightest page was turned to me,
  And naught I read of doubts or fears.

We met—we loved—one year ago,
  Beneath the stars of summer skies ;
Alas ! I knew not then, as now,
  The darkness of life's mysteries.

You took my hand—one year ago,
  Beneath the azure dome above,
And gazing on the stars you told
  The trembling story of your love.

I gave to you—one year ago,
  The only jewel that was mine ;
My heart took off her lonely crown,
  And all her riches gave to thine.

You loved me, too, when first we met,
  Your tender kisses told me so.
How changed you are from what you were
  In life and love—one year ago.

With mocking words and cold neglect,
  My truth and passion are repaid,
And of a soul, once fresh with love,
  A dreary desert you have made.

Why did you fill my youthful life
  With such wild dreams of hope and bliss?
Why did you say you loved me then,
  If it were all to end in this?

You robbed me of my faith and trust
  In all Life's beauty—Love and Truth,
You left me nothing—nothing save
  A hopeless, blighted, dreamless youth.

Strike if you will, and let the stroke
  Be heavy as my weight of woe;
I shall not shrink, my heart is cold,
  'Tis broken since one year ago.

GENIUS.

"Where'er there's a life to be kindled by love,
 Wherever a soul to inspire,
Strike this key-note of God that trembles above
 Night's silver-tongued voices of fire."

GENIUS is power.

The power that grasps in the universe, that dives out beyond space, and grapples with the starry worlds of heaven.

If genius achieves nothing, shows us no results, it is so much the less genius.

The man who is constantly fearing a lion in his path is a coward.

The man or woman whom excessive caution holds back from striking the anvil with earnest endeavor, is poor and cowardly of purpose.

The required step must be taken to reach the goal, though a precipice be the result.

Work must be done, and the result left to God.

The soul that is in earnest, will not stop to count the cost.

Circumstances cannot control genius : it will nestle with them : its power will bend and break them to its path.

This very audacity is divine.

63

Jesus of Nazareth did not ask the consent of the high priests in the temple when he drove out the "money-changers ;" but, impelled by inspiration, he knotted the cords and drove them hence.

Genius will find room for itself, or it is none.

Men and women, in all grades of life, do their utmost.

If they do little, it is because they have no capacity to do more.

I hear people speak of "unfortunate genius," of "poets who never penned their inspirations ;" that

> " Some mute inglorious Milton here may rest ;"

of "unappreciated talent," and "malignant stars," and other contradictory things.

It is all nonsense.

Where power exists, it cannot be suppressed any more than the earthquake can be smothered.

As well attempt to seal up the crater of Vesuvius as to hide God's given power of the soul.

> "You may as well forbid the mountain pines
> To wag their high tops, and to make no noise
> When they are fretten with the gusts of heaven,"

as to hush the voice of genius.

There is no such thing as unfortunate genius.

If a man or woman is fit for work, God appoints the field.

He does more ; He points to the earth with her mountains, oceans, and cataracts, and says to man, "*Be great !*"

He points to the eternal dome of heaven and its blazing worlds, and says : " Bound out thy life with beauty."

He points to the myriads of down-trodden, suffering men and women, and says : " Work with me for the redemption of these, my children."

He lures, and incites, and thrusts greatness upon men, and they will not take the gift.

Genius, on the contrary, loves toil, impediment, and poverty ; for from these it gains its strength, throws off the shadows, and lifts its proud head to immortality.

Neglect is but the fiat to an undying future.

To be popular is to be endorsed in the To-day and forgotten in the To-morrow.

It is the mess of pottage that alienates the birthright.

Genius that succumbs to misfortune, that allows itself to be blotted by the slime of slander—and other serpents that infest society—is so much the less genius.

The weak man or woman who stoops to whine over neglect, and poverty, and the snarls of the world, gives the sign of his or her own littleness.

Genius is power.

The eternal power that can silence worlds with its voice, and battle to the death ten thousand arméd Hercules.

Then make way for this God-crowned Spirit of Night, that was born in that Continuing City, but lives in lowly and down-trodden souls !

Fling out the banner !

Its broad folds of sunshine will wave over turret and dome, and over the thunder of oceans on to eternity.

5

"Fling it out, fling it out o'er the din of the world!
　Make way for this banner of flame,
That streams from the mast-head of ages unfurled,
　And inscribed by the deathless in name.
And thus through the years of eternity's flight,
　This insignia of soul shall prevail,
The centre of glory, the focus of light;
　O Genius! proud Genius, all hail!"

DRIFTS THAT BAR MY DOOR.

I.

O ANGELS! will ye never sweep the drifts from my door?

Will ye never wipe the gathering rust from the hinges?

How long must I plead and cry in vain?

Lift back the iron bars, and lead me hence.

Is there not a land of peace beyond my door?

Oh, lead me to it—give me rest—release me from this unequal strife.

Heaven can attest that I fought bravely when the heavy blows fell fast.

Was it my sin that strength failed?

Was it my sin that the battle was in vain?

Was it my sin that I lost the prize? I do not sorrow for all the bitter pain and blood it cost me.

Why do ye stand sobbing in the sunshine?

I cannot weep.

There is no sunlight in this dark cell. I am starving for light.

O angels! sweep the drifts away—unbar my door!

II.

Oh, is this all?

Is there nothing more of life?

See how dark and cold my cell.
The pictures on the walls are covered with mould.
The earth-floor is slimy with my wasting blood.
The embers are smouldering in the ashes.
The lamp is dimly flickering, and will soon starve for oil in this horrid gloom.
My wild eyes paint shadows on the walls.
And I hear the poor ghost of my lost love moaning and sobbing without.
Shrieks of my unhappiness are borne to me on the wings of the wind.
I sit cowering in fear, with my tattered garments close around my choking throat.
I move my pale lips to pray; but my soul has lost her wonted power.
Faith is weak.
Hope has laid her whitened corse upon my bosom.
The lamp sinks lower and lower. O angels! sweep the drifts away—unbar my door!

III.

Angels, is this my reward?
Is this the crown ye promised to set down on the foreheads of the loving—the suffering—the deserted?
Where are the sheaves I toiled for?
Where the golden grain ye promised?
These are but withered leaves.
Oh, is this all?
Meekly I have toiled and spun the fleece.
All the work ye assigned, my willing hands have accomplished.

See how thin they are, and how they bleed.

Ah me! what meagre pay, e'en when the task is over!

My fainting child, whose golden head graces e'en this dungeon, looks up to me and pleads for life.

O God! my heart is breaking!

Despair and Death have forced their skeleton forms through the grated window of my cell, and stand clamoring for their prey.

The lamp is almost burnt out.

Angels, sweep the drifts away—unbar my door!

IV.

Life is a lie, and Love a cheat.

There is a graveyard in my poor heart—dark, heaped-up graves, from which no flowers spring.

The walls are so high, that the trembling wings of birds do break ere they reach the summit, and they fall, wounded, and die in my bosom.

I wander 'mid the gray old tombs, and talk with the ghosts of my buried hopes.

They tell me of my Eros, and how they fluttered around him, bearing sweet messages of my love, until one day, with his strong arm, he struck them dead at his feet.

Since then, these poor lonely ghosts have haunted me night and day, for it was I who decked them in my crimson heart-tides, and sent them forth in chariots of fire.

Every breath of wind bears me their shrieks and groans.

I hasten to their graves, and tear back folds and folds

of their shrouds, and try to pour into their cold, nerveless veins the quickening tide of life once more.

Too late—too late!

Despair hath driven back Death, and clasps me in his black arms.

And the lamp! See, the lamp is dying out!

O angels! sweep the drifts from my door!—lift up the bars!

V.

Oh, let me sleep.

I close my weary eyes to think—to dream.

Is this what dreams are woven of?

I stand on the brink of a precipice, with my shivering child strained to my bare bosom.

A yawning chasm lies below. My trembling feet are on the brink.

I hear again *his* voice; but he reacheth not out his hand to save me.

Why can I not move my lips to pray?

They are cold.

My soul is dumb, too.

Death hath conquered!

I feel his icy fingers moving slowly along my heart-strings.

How cold and stiff!

The ghosts of my dead hopes are closing around me.

They stifle me.

They whisper that Eros has come back to me.

But I only see a skeleton wrapped in blood-stained cerements.

There are no lips to kiss me back to life.

O ghosts of Love, move back—give me air!

Ye smell of the dusty grave.

Ye have pressed your cold hands upon my eyes until they are eclipsed.

The lamp has burnt out.

O angels! be quick! Sweep the drifts away!—unbar my door!

Oh, light! light!

ASPIRATION.

POOR, impious Soul! that fixes its high hopes
  In the dim distance, on a throne of clouds,
And from the morning's mist would make the ropes
  To draw it up amid acclaim of crowds—
Beware!   That soaring path is lined with shrouds ;
  And he who braves it, though of sturdy breath,
May meet, half way, the avalanche and death !

O poor young Soul !—whose year-devouring glance
  Fixes in ecstasy upon a star,
Whose feverish brilliance looks a part of earth,
  Yet quivers where the feet of angels are,
And seems the future crown in realms afar—
  Beware !   A spark *thou* art, and dost but see
Thine own reflection in Eternity !

72

MISERIMUS.

"Sounding through the silent dimness
Where I faint and weary lay,
Spake a poet: 'I will lead thee
To the land of song to-day.'"

I.

O BARDS! weak heritors of passion and of pain!
Dwellers in the shadowy Palace of Dreams!
With your unmated souls flying insanely at the stars!
Why have you led me lonely and desolate to the Death-less Hill of Song?

You promised that I should ring trancing shivers of rapt melody down to the dumb earth.

You promised that its echoes should vibrate till Time's circles met in old Eternity.

You promised that I should gather the stars like blossoms to my white bosom.

You promised that I should create a new moon of Poesy.

You promised that the wild wings of my soul should shimmer through the dusky locks of the clouds, like burning arrows, down into the deep heart of the dim world.

But, O Bards! sentinels on the Lonely Hill, why breaks there yet no Day to me?

73

II.

O lonely watchers for the Light ! how long must I grope with my dead eyes in the sand ?

Only the red fire of Genius, that narrows up life's chances to the black path that crawls on to the dizzy clouds.

The wailing music that spreads its pinions to the tremble of the wind, has crumbled off to silence.

From the steep ideal the quivering soul falls in its lonely sorrow like an unmated star from the blue heights of Heaven into the dark sea.

O Genius ! is this thy promise ?

O Bards ! is this all ?

A MEMORY.

I SEE her yet, that dark-eyed one,
   Whose bounding heart God folded up
In His, as shuts when day is done,
   'Upon the elf the blossom's cup.
On many an hour like this we met,
   And as my lips did fondly greet her,
I blessed her as love's amulet :
   Earth hath no treasure, dearer, sweeter.

The stars that look upon the hill,
   And beckon from their homes at night,
Are soft and beautiful, yet still
   Not equal to her eyes of light.
They have the liquid glow of earth,
   The sweetness of a summer even,
As if some Angel at their birth
   Had dipped them in the hues of Heaven.

They may not seem to others sweet,
   Nor radiant with the beams above,
When first their soft, sad glances meet
   The eyes of those not born for love ;
Yet when on me their tender beams
   Are turned, beneath love's wide control,
Each soft, sad orb of beauty seems
   To look through mine into my soul.

I see her now that dark-eyed one,
   Whose bounding heart God folded up
In His, as shuts when day is done,
   Upon the elf the blossom's cup.
Too late we met, the burning brain,
   The aching heart alone can tell,
How filled our souls of death and pain
   When came the last, sad word, *Farewell!*

HEMLOCK IN THE FURROWS.

I.

O CROWNLESS soul of Ishmael!
Uplifting and unfolding the white tent of dreams against the sunless base of eternity!

Looking up through thy dumb desolation for white hands to reach out over the shadows, downward, from the golden bastions of God's eternal Citadel!

Praying for Love to unloose the blushing bindings of his nimble shaft and take thee up to his fullest fruition!

Poor Soul! hast thou no prophecy to gauge the distance betwixt thee and thy crown?

Thy crown?

Alas! there is none.

Only a golden-rimmed shadow that went before thee, marking in its tide barren shoals and dust.

At last resting its bright length down in the valley of tears.

Foolish soul! let slip the dusty leash.

Cease listening along the borders of a wilderness for the lost echoes of life.

Drift back through the scarlet light of Memory into the darkness once more.

A corpse hath not power to feel the tying of its hands.

77

II.

To-night, O Soul! shut off thy little rimmings of Hope, and let us go back to our hemlock that sprang up in the furrows.

Let us go back with bleeding feet and try to break up the harvestless ridges where we starved.

Let us go down to the black sunset whose wings of fire burnt out thy flowery thickets of Day, and left a Night to swoop down the lonesome clouds to thee.

Go back to the desolate time when the dim stars looked out from Heaven, filmy and blank, like eyes in the wide front of some dead beast.

Go, press thy nakedness to the burnt, bare rocks, under whose hot, bloodless ribs the River of Death runs black with human sorrow.

To-night, O Soul! fly back through all the grave-yards of thy Past.

Fly back to them this night with thy fretful wings, even though their bloody breadth must wrestle long against Hell's hollow bosom!

III.

Jealous Soul!

The stars that are trembling forth their silent messages to the hills have none for thee!

The mother-moon that so lovingly reacheth down her arms of light heedeth not thy Love!

See, the pale pinions that thou hast pleaded for gather themselves up into rings and then slant out to the dust!

The passion-flowers lift up their loving faces and open

their velvet lips to the baptism of Love, but heed not thy
warm kisses!

Shut out all this brightness that hath God's Beauty and
liveth back the silence of His Rest.

Cease knocking at the starry gate of the wondrous
realm of Song.

Hush away this pleading and this praying.

Go back to thy wail of fetter and chain!

Go back to thy night of loving in vain!

IV.

O weak Soul! let us follow the heavy hearse that bore
our old Dream out past the white-horned Daylight of
Love.

Let thy pale Dead come up from their furrows of
winding-sheets to mock thy prayers with what thy days
might have been.

Let the Living come back and point out the shadows
they swept o'er the disk of thy morning star.

Have thou speech with them for the story of its swim-
ming down in tremulous nakedness to the Red Sea of
the Past.

Go back and grapple with thy lost Angels that stand in
terrible judgment against thee.

Seek thou the bloodless skeleton once hugged to thy
depths.

Hath it grown warmer under thy passionate kissings?

Or, hath it closed its seeming wings and shrunk its
white body down to a glistening coil?

Didst thou wait the growth of fangs to front the arrows
of Love's latest peril?

Didst thou not see a black, hungry vulture wheeling down low to the white-bellied coil where thy Heaven had once based itself?

O blind Soul of mine!

V.

Blind, blind with tears!

Not for thee shall Love climb the Heaven of thy columned Hopes to Eternity!

Under the silver shadow of the cloud waits no blushing star thy tryst.

Didst thou not see the pale, widowed West loose her warm arms and slide the cold burial earth down upon the bare face of thy sun?

Gazing upon a shoal of ashes, thou hast lost the way that struck upon the heavy, obstructive valves of the grave to thy Heaven.

Mateless thou needs must vaguely feel along the dark, cold steeps of Night.

Hath not suffering made thee wise?

When, oh when?

VI.

Go down to the black brink of Death and let its cool waters press up to thy weary feet.

See if its trembling waves will shatter the grand repeating of thy earth-star.

See if the eyes that said to thee their speechless Love so close will reach thee from this sorrowful continent of Life.

See if the red hands that seamed thy shroud will come around thy grave.

Then, O Soul! thou mayst drag them to the very edges of the Death-pit, and shake off their red shadows!

Thy strong vengeance may then bind the black-winged crew down level with their beds of fire!

VII.

But wait, wait!

Take up the ruined cup of Life that struck like a planet through the dark, and shone clear and full as we starved for the feast within.

Go down to the black offings of the Noiseless Sea, and wait, poor Soul!

Measure down the depth of thy bitterness and wait!

Bandage down with the grave-clothes the pulses of thy dying life and wait!

Wail up thy wild, desolate echoes to the pitying arms of God and wait!

Wait, wait!

6

HEAR, O ISRAEL!

(From the Hebrew.)

"And they shall be my people, and I will be their God."—Jeremiah
xxxii. 38.

I.

HEAR, O Israel! and plead my cause against the
ungodly nation!
'Midst the terrible conflict of Love and Peace, I de-
parted from thee, my people, and spread my tent of many
colors in the land of Egypt.
In their crimson and fine linen I girded my white form.
Sapphires gleamed their purple light from out the dark-
ness of my hair.
The silver folds of their temple foot-cloth was spread
beneath my sandaled feet.
Thus I slumbered through the daylight.

Slumbered 'midst the vapor of sin,
Slumbered 'midst the battle and din,
Wakened 'midst the strangle of breath,
Wakened 'midst the struggle of death!

II.

Hear, O Israel! my people—to thy goodly tents do I
return with unstained hands.

Like as the harts for the water-brooks, in thirst, do pant and bray, so pants and cries my longing soul for the house of Jacob.

My tears have unto me been meat, both in night and day :

And the crimson and fine linen moulders in the dark tents of the enemy.

With bare feet and covered head do I return to thee, O Israel !

With sackcloth have I bound the hem of my garments.

With olive leaves have I trimmed the border of my bosom.

The breaking waves did pass o'er me ; yea, were mighty in their strength—

Strength of the foe's oppression.

My soul was cast out upon the waters of Sin : but it has come back to me.

My transgressions have vanished like a cloud.

The curse of Balaam hath turned to a blessing ;

And the doors of Jacob turn not on their hinges against me.

Rise up, O Israel ! for it is I who passed through the fiery furnace seven times, and come forth unscathed, to re-deem thee from slavery, O my nation ! and lead thee back to God.

III.

Brothers mine, fling out your white banners over this Red Sea of wrath !

Hear ye not the Death-cry of a thousand burning, bleeding wrongs ?

Against the enemy lift thy sword of fire, even thou, O Israel! whose prophet I am.

For I, of all thy race, with these tear-blinded eyes, still see the watch-fire leaping up its blood-red flame from the ramparts of our Jerusalem!

And my heart alone beats and palpitates, rises and falls with the glimmering and the gleaming of the golden beacon flame, by whose light I shall lead thee, O my people! back to freedom!

Give me time—oh give me time to strike from your brows the shadow-crowns of Wrong!

On the anvil of my heart will I rend the chains that bind ye.

Look upon me—oh look upon me, as I turn from the world—from love, and passion, to lead thee, thou Chosen of God, back to the pastures of Right and Life!

Fear me not; for the best blood that heaves this heart now runs for thee, thou Lonely Nation!

Why wear ye not the crown of eternal royalty, that God set down upon your heads?

Back, tyrants of the red hands!

Slouch back to your ungodly tents, and hide the Cain-brand on your foreheads!

Life for life, blood for blood, is the lesson ye teach us.

We, the Children of Israel, will not creep to the kennel graves ye are scooping out with iron hands, like scourged hounds!

Israel! rouse ye from the slumber of ages, and, though Hell welters at your feet, carve a road through these tyrants!

The promised dawn-light is here ; and God—O the God of our nation is calling !

Press on—press on !

IV.

Ye, who are kings, princes, priests, and prophets. Ye men of Judah and bards of Jerusalem, hearken unto my voice, and I will speak thy name, O Israel !

Fear not ; for God hath at last let loose His thinkers, and their voices now tremble in the mighty depths of this old world !

Rise up from thy blood-stained pillows !

Cast down to dust the hideous, galling chains that bind thy strong hearts down to silence !

Wear ye the badge of slaves ?

See ye not the watch-fire ?

Look aloft, from thy wilderness of thought !

Come forth with the signs and wonders, and thy strong hands, and stretched-out arms, even as thou didst from Egypt !

Courage, courage ! trampled hearts !

Look at these pale hands and frail arms, that have rent asunder the welded chains that an army of the Philistines bound about me !

But the God of all Israel set His seal of fire on my breast, and lighted up, with inspiration, the soul that pants for the Freedom of a nation !

With eager wings she fluttered above the blood-stained bayonet-points of the millions, who are trampling upon the strong throats of God's people.

Rise up, brave hearts !

The sentry cries : " All's well !" from Hope's tower !
Fling out your banners of Right !
The watch fire grows brighter !
  All's well ! All's well !
  Courage ! Courage !
The Lord of Hosts is in the field,
The God of Jacob is our shield !

WHERE THE FLOCKS SHALL BE LED.

WHERE shall I lead the flocks to-day?

Is there no Horeb for me beyond this desert?

Is there no rod with which I can divide this sea of blood to escape mine enemies?

Must I pine in bondage and drag these heavy chains through the rocky path of my unrecompensed toil?

Must I, with these pale, feeble hands, still lift the wreathed bowl for others to drink, while my lips are parched and my soul unslaked?

Must I hold the light above my head that others may find the green pastures as they march in advance, whilst I moan and stumble with my bare feet tangled and clogged with this load of chains?

Must I still supply the lamp with oil that gives no light to me?

Shall I reck not my being's wane in these long days of bondage and struggle?

Is there no time for me to pray?

Others are climbing the hill-side of glory whilst I am left to wrestle with darkness in the valley below.

Oh where shall I lead the flocks to-day?

Once the soft white flowers of love bloomed upon my bosom.

But, oh! see this iron crown hath crushed the purple blood from my temples until the roses are drowned in it and 'tis withered and weeping on my breast.

The dear hands that planted the sweet flowers should not have been the ones to clasp this heavy iron band round my aching head.

Oh why is it that those we love and cling to with the deepest adoration of our unschooled natures should be the first to whet the steel and bury it in the warm blood that passionate love had created?

Answer me, ye who are ranged mockingly around me with your unsheathed knives.   Answer me.

I know that ye are waiting to strike, but answer me first.

I know that if my tearful eyes do but wander from ye one moment, your trembling cowardly hands will strike the blow that your black souls are crying out for.

But let your haggard lips speak to give me warning.

Ye wait to see if these tears will blind me.

But I shall not plead for mercy.

Weak and fainting as I am, I fear you not.

For, lo! behold!

I bare to you my white mother bosom!

See, I draw from my heart a dagger whose blade is keener than any ye can hold against me.

The hands I loved most whetted it, and struck with fatal precision ye never can, for he knew where the heart lay.

No one else can ever know.

Look how the thick blood slowly drips from the point of the blade and sinks into the sand at my feet.

The white sand rolls over and covers the stains.

Flowers will spring up even there.

One day the sands will loose their seal, and they will speak.

The first shall be last and the last shall be first.

The first is my own life and the last my child.

That one will bloom eternally.

And together we will sound the horn that shall herd the flocks and lead them up to the Father's pastures.

For I know that somewhere there grows a green bush in the crevice of a rock, and that the enemy's foot may not crush it nor his hand uproot it.

A golden gate shall be unloosed, and we shall feed upon the freshness of the mountains.

But, see, the furnace has been heated seven times.

I still stand barefoot and bondage-bound, girt around my warriors, and chained and down-trodden upon these burning sands.

And yet I will escape.

Look, the pillar of cloud is over my head.

He who saved the bush on Horeb from the flames can lead me through the Red Sea, beyond the reach of these Egyptians with their rumbling chariots, tramping steeds, clashing weapons, and thunders of war.

Above the tumult I hear the voice of Aaron.

When the sun rises the chains shall be unsealed.

The blood shall be lifted from the earth and will speak.

The task-masters shall perish.

The white flocks shall be led back to the broad plains of Hebron.

I still see the pillar of cloud.

God is in the midst of us !

PRO PATRIA.

AMERICA, 1861.

GOD'S armies of Heaven, with pinions extended,
  Spread wide their white arms to the standard of
    Light;
And bending far down to the great Heart of Nature,
  With kisses of Love drew us up from the Night.

Proud soul of the Bondless! whose stars fleck with crim-
    son,
  And warm dreams of gold ev'ry pillar and dome,
That strengthens and crowns the fair temples upswelling
  To glitter, far-seen, in our Liberty's home—

The spirits of Heroes and Sires of the People,
  Leaned down from the battlements guarding the world;
To breathe for your Destiny omens of glory
  And freedom eternal, in Honor impearled.

The storm-goaded mountains, and trees that had battled
  With winds sweeping angrily down through the years,
Turned red in the blood of the roses of Heaven,
  'Neath fires lit by sunset on vanishing spears.

The soft Beam of Peace bronzed the rocks of stern ages,
  And crept from the valley to burn on the spire;

And stooped from the glimmer of gems in the palace,
    To glow in the hovel a soul-heating fire.

Each turret, and terrace, and archway of grandeur,
    Its beauty up-rounded through laughs of the light;
And world-crown'd America chose for her standard
    The blush of the Day and the eyes of the Night.

Then Liberty's sceptre, its last jewel finding,
    Was waved by a God o'er the years to be born,
And far in the future there rusted and crumbled
    The chains of the centuries, ne'er to be worn.

The wave-hosts patrolling the sullen Atlantic,
    With helmets of snow, and broad silvery shields,
Ran clamoring up to the seed-sown embrasures,
    And fashioned new dews for the buds of the fields:

They spread their scroll shields for the breast of Columbia,
    And turned their storm-swords to the enemy's fleet;
Their glory to humble the tyrant that braved them,
    Their honor to lave fair America's feet!

No hot hand of Mars scattered red bolts of thunder
    From out the blest land on their message-wind's breath;
But softly the murmur of Peace wantoned o'er them,
    And soothed War to sleep in the Cradle of Death,

Then hiding their snow plumes, they slept in their armor,
    And as the sun shone on their crystalline mail;
Lo! Freedom beheld, from her mountains, a mirror,
    And caught her own image spread under a sail!

So, blest was Columbia ; the focus of Nature's
  Best gifts, and the dimple where rested God's smile ;
The Queen of the World in her young strength and beauty,
  The pride of the skies in her freedom from guile.

Aloft on the mount of God's liberty endless,
  Half-veiled by the clouds of His temple she stood,
Arrayed in the glory of Heaven, the mortal,
  With vigor Immortal unchained in her blood.

A bright helm of stars on her white brow was seated,
  And gold were the plumes from its clusters that fell
To light the gaunt faces of slaves in old kingdoms,
  And show them the way to the hand they loved well.

No gorget of steel rested on her bare bosom,
  Where glittered a necklace of gems from the skies ;
And girding her waist was the red band of sunset,
  With light intertwined 'neath the glance of her eyes.

The sword that had bridged in the dark time of trouble,
  Her heart's grand Niagara rolling in blood ;
Still sheathless she held ; but it turned to a sunbeam,
  And blessed what it touched, like a finger of God !

The robes of her guardian Angels swept round her,
  And flashed through the leaves of the grand Tree of
    Life,
Till all the sweet birds in its depths woke to music,
  And e'en the bruised limbs with new being were rife.

The Eagle's gray eyes, from the crag by the ocean,
  Undazed by the sun, saw the vision of love, *

And swift on the rim of the shield of Columbia,
  The bold Eagle fell from the white throne of Jove !

Columbia ! My Country ! My Mother ! thy glory
  Was born in a spirit Immortal, divine ;
And when from God's lips passed the nectar of heaven,
  Thy current baptismal was deified wine !

Thou born of Eternal ! the hand that would harm thee
  Must wither to dust, and in dust be abhorred,
For thine is the throne whose blue canopy muffles
  The footfalls of angels, the steps of the Lord !

But hush ! 'Twas the flap of the raven's dark pinions
  That sounded in woe on the breeze as it passed ;
There cometh a hum, as of distance-veiled battle,
  From out the deep throat of the quivering blast ;

There cometh a sound like the moan of a lost one
  From out the red jaws of Hell's cavern of Death ;
The Eagle's strong wing feels the talon of Discord,
  And all the fair sunlight goes out with a breath !

And see how the purple-hued hills and the valleys
  Are dark with bent necks and with arms all unnerved ;
And black, yelling hounds bay the soul into madness—
  The Huntsman of Hell drives the pack that has swerved !

The pale steeds of Death shake the palls of their saddles,
  And spread their black manes, wrought of shrouds, to
    the wind,
The curst sons of Discord each courser bestriding,
  To guide the Arch-Demon, who lingers behind.

They thunder in rage, o'er the red path of Battle,
  Far up the steep mount where fair Liberty keeps
The soul of a Tyrant in parchment imprisoned;
  God pity us all, if her Sentinel sleeps!

Our Father in Heaven! the shadow of fetters
  Is held in the shade of the Dove's little wing;
And must it again on our smothered hearts settle?
  Peace slain—and the knell of our Honor they ring!

Behold! from the night-checkered edge of the woodland
  A wall of red shields crowdeth into the land,
Their rims shooting horror and bloody confusion,
  Their fields spreading darkness on every hand.

A forest of morions utter grim murder—
  Threats kissed by the sun from their long tongues of steel;
Lo, forests of spears hedge the heart of Columbia,
  And soon their keen points her fair bosom may feel!

Her Cain-branded foes! How they crawl in the valley,
  And creep o'er the hills, in their dastardly fear!
Afraid, lest their victim should suddenly waken
  And blast them for e'er with a womanly tear!

Like hunters who compass the African jungle,
  Where slumbers Numidia's lion by day,
They falter and pale, looking back at each other,
  And some, in their falsehood, to Providence pray!

Assassins of Liberty! comes there not o'er you
  A thought of the time, when the land you would blight,

Though slumbering 'mid tombs of a hundred dead nations,
  Though Britain's steel bulwarks broke into the light?

And can ye forget the hot blood-rain that deluged
  The Hearts of the Fathers, who left to your care
The beautiful Trust now in slumber before you,
  They starved, fought, and fell to preserve from a snare?

Would ye splash, in your madness, the blood of the children,
  With merciless blows, in the poor mother's face?
Turn back, ye Assassins! or wear on your foreheads
  For ever the brand of a God-hated race!

Down, down to the dust with ye, cowards inhuman!
  And learn, as ye grovel, for mercy to live,
That Love is the Sceptre and Throne of the Nation,
  And Freedom the Crown that the centuries give!

Unrighteous Ambition has slept in our limits
  Since fearless Columbia sheathed her bright blade:
And at her dread Vengeance on those who awake it,
  The soul of the stoutest might well be dismayed.

Beware! for the spirit of God's Retribution
  Will make a red sunrise when Liberty dies;
The Traitors shall writhe in the glow of a morning,
  And drown in the blood that is filling their eyes!

The bright blade of old, when it leaps from the scabbard
  Like Lightning shall fall on the traitorous head,
And hurl with each stroke, in its world-shock of thunder,
  A thrice cursed soul to the deeps of the Dead!

Beware ! for when once ye have made your Red Ocean,
　　Its waves shall rise up with tempestuous swell,
And hurl your stained souls, like impurities, from them
　　Up death's dark slope, to the skull beach of Hell !

KARAZAH TO KARL.

COME back to me ! my life is young,
   My soul is scarcely on her way,
And all the starry songs she's sung,
   Are prelude to a grander lay.
                Come back to me !

Let this song-born soul receive thee,
   Glowing its fondest truth to prove ;
Why so early did'st thou leave me,
   Are our heaven-grand life of love ?
                Come back to me !

My burning lips shall set their seal
   On our betrothal bond to-night,
While whispering murmurs will reveal
   How souls can love in God's own light.
                Come back to me !

Come back to me ! The stars will be
   Silent witnesses of our bliss,
And all the past shall seem to thee
   But a sweet dream to herald this !
                Come back to me !

A FRAGMENT.

"Oh! I am sick of what I am. Of all
Which I in life can ever hope to be.
Angels of light be pitiful to me."

THE cold chain of life presseth heavily on me to-
night.

The thundering pace of thought is curbed, and, like a
fiery steed, dasheth against the gloomy walls of my pris-
oned soul.

Oh! how long will my poor thoughts lament their nar-
row faculty? When will the rein be loosed from my im-
patient soul?

Ah! then I will climb the blue clouds and dash down
to dust those jeweled stars, whose silent light wafts a
mocking laugh to the poor musician who sitteth before
the muffled organ of my great hopes. With a hand of
fire he toucheth the golden keys. All breathless and rapt
I list for an answer to his sweet meaning, but the glitter-
ing keys give back only a faint hollow sound—the echo of
a sigh!

Cruel stars to mock me with your laughing light!

Oh! see ye not the purple life-blood ebbing from my
side?

But ye heed it not—and I scorn ye all.

Foolish stars! Ye forget that this strong soul will one day be loosed.

I will have ye in my power yet, I'll meet ye on the grand door of old eternity.

Ah! then ye will not laugh, but shrink before me like very beggars of light that ye are, and I will grasp from your gleaming brows the jeweled crown, rend away your glistening garments, and hold ye up blackened skeletons for the laugh and scorn of all angels, and then drive ye out to fill this horrid space of darkness that I now grovel in.

But, alas! I am weary, sick, and faint.

The chains do bind the shrinking flesh too close.

"Angels of light, be pitiful to me."

Oh! this life, after all, is but a promise—a poor promise, that is too heavy to bear—heavy with blood, reeking human blood. The atmosphere is laden with it. When I shut my eyes it presses so close to their lids that I must gasp and struggle to open them.

I know that the sins of untrue hearts are clogging up the air-passages of the world, and that we, who love and suffer, will soon be smothered, and in this terrible darkness too.

For me—my poor lone, deserted body—I care not. I am not in favor of men's eyes.

" Nor am I skilled immortal stuff to weave.
No rose of honor wear I on my sleeve."

But the soft silver hand of death will unbind the galling

bands that clasp the fretting soul in her narrow prison-house, and she may then escape the iron hands that would crush the delicate fibres to dust.

O soul, where are thy wings? Have they with their rude hands torn them from thy mutilated form? We must creep slowly and silently away through the midnight darkness. But we are strong yet, and can battle with the fiends who seek to drive us back to the river of blood.

But, alas! it is so late, and I am alone—alone listening to the gasps and sighs of a weary soul beating her broken wing against the darkened walls of her lonely cell.

> "My labor is a vain and empty strife,
>   A useless tugging at the wheels of life."

Shall I still live—filling no heart, working no good, and the cries of my holy down-trodden race haunting me? Beseeching me—me, with these frail arms and this poor chained soul, to lift them back to their birthright of glory.

> "Angels of light, be pitiful to me."

I have wearied Heaven with my tears and prayers till I have grown pale and old, but a shadow of my former self, and all for power, blessed power! Not for myself—but for those dearer and worthier than I—those from out whose hearts my memory has died for ever.

But, alas! it is vain.

Prayers and tears will not bring back sweet hope and love.

I may still sigh and weep for these soft-winged nestling

angels of my lost dreams till I am free to seek them in the grand homes where I have housed them with the golden-haired son of the sky.

It is midnight, and the world is still battling—the weak are falling, the strong and the wrong are exulting.

And I, like the dying stag, am hunted down to the ocean border, still asking for peace and rest of the great gleaming eyes that pierce the atmosphere of blood and haunt me with their pleading looks. Whispers are there —low, wailing whispers from white-browed children as though I could bear their chained souls o'er Charon's mystic river of their purple blood.

Alas! star after star has gone down till not one is in sight. How dark and cold it is growing!

Oh, light! why have you fled to a fairer land and left

> " An unrigged hulk, to rot upon life's ford—
> The crew of mutinous senses overboard?"

It is too late. I faint with fear of these atom-fiends that do cling to my garments in this darkness.

Oh! rest for thee, my weary soul,
    The coil is round thee all too fast.
Too close to earth thy pinions clasp:
    A trance-like death hath o'er thee past.

Oh, soul! oh, broken soul, arise,
    And plume thee for a prouder flight.
In vain, in vain—'tis sinking now
    And dying in eternal night.

" Suffer and be still."

Death will bind up thy powerful wings, and to the organ music of my great hopes thou shalt beat sublimer airs.

Wait until eternity.

THE AUTOGRAPH ON THE SOUL.

IN the Beginning, God, the great Schoolmaster, wrote upon the white leaves of our souls the text of life, in His own autograph.

Upon all souls it has been written alike.

We set forth with the broad, fair characters penned in smoothness and beauty, and promise to bear them back so, to the Master, who will endorse them with eternal life.

But, alas! how few of us can return with these copy-books unstained and unblotted?

Man—the school-boy Man—takes a jagged pen and dips it in blood, and scrawls line after line of his hopeless, shaky, weak-backed, spattering imitation of the unattainable flourish and vigor of the autograph at the top of our souls.

And thus they go on, in unweary reiteration, until the fair leaves are covered with unseemly blots, and the Schoolmaster's copy is no longer visible.

No wonder, then, that we shrink and hide, and play truant as long as we possibly can, before handing in to the Master our copy-books for examination.

How soiled with the dust of men, and stained with the blood of the innocent, some of these books are!

Surely, some will look fairer than others.

Those of the lowly and despised of men ;
The wronged and the persecuted ;
The loving and the deserted ;
The suffering and the despairing ;
The weak and the struggling ;
The desolate and the oppressed ;
The authors of good books ;
The defenders of women ;
The mothers of new-born children ;
The loving wives of cruel husbands ;
The strong throats that are choked with their own blood,
and cannot cry out the oppressor's wrong.

On the souls of these of God's children of inspiration,
His autograph will be handed up to the judgment-seat, on
the Day of Examination, pure and unsoiled.

The leaf may be torn, and traces of tears, that fell as
prayers went up, may dim the holy copy, but its fair,
sharp, and delicate outlines will only gleam the stronger,
and prove the lesson of life, that poor, down-trodden hu-
manity has been studying for ages and ages—the eternal
triumph of mind over matter !

What grand poems these starving souls will be, after
they are signed and sealed by the Master-hand !

But what of the oppressor ?

What of the betrayer ?

What of him that holds a deadly cup, that the pure of
heart may drink ?

What of fallen women, who are covered with paint and
sin, and flaunt in gaudy satins, never heeding the black
stains within their own breasts ?—lost to honor, lost to
themselves ; glittering in jewels and gold ; mingling with

sinful men, who, with sneering looks and scoffing laughs, drink wine beneath the gas-light's glare.

Wrecks of womanly honor !

Wrecks of womanly souls !

Wrecks of life and love !

Blots that deface the fair earth with crime and sin !

Fallen—fallen so low that the cries and groans of the damned must sometimes startle their death-signed hearts, as they flaunt through the world, with God's curse upon them !

What of the money-makers, with their scorching days and icy nights ?

Their hollow words and ghastly smiles ?

Their trifling deceits ?

Their shameless lives ?

Their starving menials ?

Their iron hands, that grasp the throats of weary, white-haired men ?

Will their coffins be black ?

They should be red—stained with the blood of their victims !

Their shrouds should be make with pockets ; and all their gold should be placed therein, to drag them deeper down than the sexton dug the grave !

How will it be with him who deceives and betrays women ?

Answer me this, ye men who have brought woe and desolation to the heart of woman ; and, by your fond lips, breathing sighs, and vows of truth and constancy—your deceit and desertion, destroyed her, body and soul !

There are more roads to the heart than by cold steel.

You drew her life and soul after you by your pretended love. Perhaps she sacrificed her home, her father and her mother—her God and her religion for you!

Perhaps for you she has endured pain and penury!

Perhaps she is the mother of your child, living and praying for you!

And how do you repay this devotion?

By entering the Eden of her soul, and leaving the trail of the serpent, that can never be erased from its flowers; for the best you trample beneath your feet, while the fairest you pluck as a toy to while away an idle hour, then dash aside for another of a fairer cast.

Then, if she plead with her tears, and her pure hands, to Heaven, that you come back to your lost honor, and to her heart, you do not hesitate to tear that suffering heart with a shameless word, that cuts like a jagged knife, and add your curse to crush her light of life!

Have ye seen the blood-stained steel, dimmed with the heart's warm blood of the suicide?

Have ye seen the pallid lips, the staring eyes, the unclosed, red-roofed mouth—the bubbling gore, welling up from a woman's breast?

Have ye seen her dying in shivering dread, with the blood dabbled o'er her bosom?

Have ye heard her choked voice rise in prayer—her pale lips breathing his name—the name of him who deceived her? Yes! a prayer coming up with the bubbling blood—a blessing on him for whom she died!

Why did she not pray for her despairing self?

O God! have mercy on the souls of men who are false to their earthly love and trust!

But the interest will come round—all will come round!
Nothing will escape the Schoolmaster's sleepless eye!
The indirect is always as great and real as the direct.
Not one word or deed—
Not one look or thought—
Not a motive but will be stamped on the programme of
our lives, and duly realized by us, and returned, and held
up to light heaven or flood hell with.
All the best actions of war or peace—
All the help given to strangers—
Cheering words to the despairing—
Open hands to the shunned—
Lifting of lowly hearts—
Teaching children of God—
Helping the widow and the fatherless—
Giving light to some desolate home—
Reading the Bible to the blind—
Protecting the defenceless—
Praying with the dying.
These are acts that need no Poet to make poems of
them ; for they will live through ages and ages, on to
Eternity. And when God opens the sealed book on the
Day of Judgment, these poems of the history of lives will
be traced in letters of purple and gold, beneath the Mas-
ter's Autograph.

ADELINA PATTI.

THOU Pleiad of the lyric world
  Where Pasta, Garcia shone,
Come back with thy sweet voice again,
  And gem the starry zone.

Though faded, still the vision sees
  The loveliest child of night,
The fairest of the Pleiades,
  Its glory and its light.

How fell with music from thy tongue
  The picture which it drew
Of Lucia, radiant, warm, and young—
  Amina, fond and true.

Or the young Marie's grace and art,
  So free from earthly strife,
Beating upon the sounding heart,
  The gay tattoo of life!

Fair Florence! home of glorious Art,
  And mistress of its sphere,
Clasp fast thy beauties to thy heart—
  Behold thy rival here!

DYING.

I.

LEAVE me ; oh ! leave me,
Lest I find this low earth sweeter than the skies.

Leave me lest I deem Faith's white bosom bared to the betraying arms of Death.

Hush your fond voice, lest it shut out the angel trumpet-call !

See my o'erwearied feet bleed for rest.

Loose the clinging and the clasping of my clammy fingers.

Your soft hand of Love may press back the dark, awful shadows of Death, but the soul faints in the strife and struggles of nights that have no days.

I am so weary with this climbing up the smooth steep sides of the grave wall.

My dimmed eyes can no longer strain up through the darkness to the temples and palaces that you have built for me upon Life's summit.

God is folding up the white tent of my youth.

My name is enrolled for the pallid army of the dead.

II.

It is too late, too late !

You may not kiss back my breath to the sunshine.

How can these trembling hands of dust reach up to bend the untempered iron of Destiny down to my woman-forehead?

Where is the wedge to split its knotty way between the Past and the Future?

The soaring bird that would sing its life out to the stars, may not leave its own atmosphere;

For, in the long dead reaches of blank space in the Beyond, its free wings fall back to earth baffled.

Once gathering all my sorrows up to one purpose—rebel-like—I dared step out into Light, when, lo! Death tied my unwilling feet, and with hands of ice, bandaged my burning lips, and set up, between my eyes and the Future, the great Infinite of Eternity, full in the blazing sun of my Hope!

From the red round life of Love I have gone down to the naked house of Fear.

Drowned in a storm of tears.

My wild wings of thought drenched from beauty to the color of the ground.

Going out at the hueless gates of day.

Dying, dying.

III.

Oh! is there no strength in sorrow, or in prayers?

Is there no power in the untried wings of the soul, to smite the brazen portals of the sun?

Must the black-sandaled foot of Night tramp out the one star that throbs through the darkness of my waning life?

May not the strong arm of " I will," bring some beam
to lead me into my sweet Hope again?

Alas, too late ! too late !

The power of these blood-dripping cerements sweeps
back the audacious thought to emptiness.

Hungry Death will not heed the poor bird that has
tangled its bright wing through my deep-heart pulses.

Moaning and living.
Dying and loving.

IV.

See the poor wounded snake ; how burdened to the
ground ;

How it lengthens limberly along the dust.

Now palpitates into bright rings only to unwind, and
reach its bleeding head up the steep high walls around us.

Now, alas ! falling heavily back into itself, quivering
with unuttered pain ;

Choking with its own blood it dies in the dust.

So we are crippled ever ;
Reaching and falling,
Silent and dying.

V.

Gold and gleaming jewel shatter off their glory well in
the robes of royalty, but when we strain against the
whelming waves, the water gurgling down our drowning
throats, we shred them off, and hug the wet, cold rocks
lovingly.

Then old death goes moaning back from the steady
footing of Life baffled.

Ah ! is it too late for me to be wise.

Will my feeble hands fail me in the moveless steppings back to the world ?

Oh ! if youth were·only back !

Oh ! if the years would only empty back their ruined days into the lap of the Present !

Oh ! if yesterday would only unravel the light it wove into the purple of the Past !

Ah ! then might I be vigilant !

Then might the battle be mine !

Nor should my sluggish blood drip down the rocks till the noon-tide sun should draw it up mistily in smoke.

Then should the heaviness of soul have dropped as trees do their weight of rainy leaves.

Nor should the sweet leash of Love have slipped from my hungry life, and left me pining, dying for his strength.

I should have wrapt up my breathing in the naked bosom of Nature, and she would have kissed me back to sweetest comfort, and I would have drawn up from her heart draughts of crusted nectar and promises of eternal joys.

Oh ! it is not the glittering garniture of God's things that come quivering into the senses, that makes our lives look white through the windings of the wilderness.

It is the soul's outflow of purple light that clashes up a music with the golden blood of strong hearts.

Souls with God's breath upon them,

Hearts with Love's light upon them.

VI.

If my weak puny hand could reach up and rend the sun

from his throne to-day, then were the same but a little thing for me to do.

It is the Far Off, the great Unattainable, that feeds the passion we feel for a star.

Looking up so high, worshiping so silently, we tramp out the hearts of flowers that lift their bright heads for us and die alone.

If only the black, steep grave gaped between us, I feel that I could over-sweep all its gulfs.

I believe that Love may unfold its white wings even in the red bosom of Hell.

I know that its truth can measure the distance to Heaven with one thought.

Then be content to let me go, for these pale hands shall reach up from the grave, and still draw the living waters of Love's well.

That is better, surer than climbing with bruised feet and bleeding hands to plead with the world for what is mine own.

Then straighten out the crumpled length of my hair, and loose all the flowers one by one.

God is not unjust.

VII.

Oh ! in the great strength of thy unhooded soul, pray for my weakness.

Let me go ! See the pale and solemn army of the night is on the march.

Do not let my shivering soul go wailing up for a human love to the throne of the Eternal.

Have we not watched the large setting sun drive a

column of light through the horizon down into the darkness?

So within the grave's night, O my beloved! shall my love burn on to eternity.

O Death! Death! loose out thy cold, stiff fingers from my quivering heart!

Let the warm blood rush back to gasp up but one more word!

O Love! thou art stronger, mightier than all!

O Death! thou hast but wedded me to Life!

Life is Love, and Love is Eternity.

SAVED.

I.

O SOLDIERS, soldiers, get ye back, I pray!
　　Hush out of sound your trampings so near his lowly head!
　　Hush back the echoes of your footfalls to the muffling distance!
　　O soldiers, wake not my sleeping love!
　　Get ye back, I pray!
　　To-morrow will he wake, and lead ye on as bravely as before.
　　To-morrow will he lift the blazing sword above a crimson flood of victory.
　　Get ye back and wait.
　　He is weary, and would sleep.

II.

　　Soft, soft, he sleepeth well.
　　Why stand ye all so stern and sad?
　　So garmented in the dust and blood of battle?
　　Why linger on the field to-day? See how the dark locks hang in bloody tangles about your glaring eyes!
　　Get ye to your silent tents, I pray!
　　See ye not your soldier-chief sleeps safe and well?

SAVED.

What say ye?
"Dead!"
O blind, blind soldiers! Should I not know?
Have I not watched him all the long, long battle?
On this cold and sunless plain my tottering feet struck the pathway to my soldier.
My loving arms have clasped him from the black, hungry jaws of Death.
With the neglected sunshine of my hair I shielded his pale face from the cannon-glare.
On my breast, as on a wave of heaven-light, have I lulled him to the soft beauty of dreams.
He has been yours to-day; he is mine now.
He has fought bravely, and would sleep.
I know, I know.

III.

O soldiers, soldiers, take him not hence!
Do not press tears back into your pitiful eyes, and say:
"His soul hath found its rest."
Why lean ye on your blood-stained spears, and point to that dark wound upon his throat?
I can kiss its pain and terror out.
Leave him, I pray ye!
He will wake to-morrow, and cheer ye in your tents at dawn.
And ye shall see him smile on her who soothes his weary head to sleep through this long night.
It was I who found him at the battle's dreadful close.
Weary and wounded, he sank to rest upon the field.

Murmuring out his tender voice, he called my name, and whispered of our love, and its sweet eternity.

'Mid brooding love and clinging kisses, his tender eyes let down their silken barriers to the day.

Their pale roofs close out the defeat, and in my arms he finds the joy of glorious victory.

IV.

O soldiers, leave him to me!

The morning, bridegroomed by the sun, cannot look down to the midnight for comfort.

In the thick front of battle I claimed what is mine own.

I saw the Grim Foe open wide his red-leafed book, but he wrote not therein the name of my brave love.

Life hath no chance that he cannot combat with a single hand.

Now he wearies from the struggling grace of a brave surrendering.

He sleeps, he sleeps.

V.

Go, soldiers, go!

I pray ye wake him not.

I have kissed his pale, cold mouth, and staunched the crimson wound upon his throat.

The mournful moon has seen my silent watch above his lonely bed.

Her pitying eyes reproached me not.

How durst yours?

Go, soldiers, go!

VI.

I charge ye by the love ye bear your sleeping chieftain, wake him not!

To-morrow he will wake, eager to wheel into battle-line.

To-morrow he will rise, and mount the steed he loveth well, and lead ye cheerily on to the attack!

To-morrow his voice will ring its Hope along your tramping troops!

But oh! wait, wait!

He is weary, and must sleep!

Go, soldiers, go!

ANSWER ME.

I.

IN from the night.
   The storm is lifting his black arms up to the sky.
Friend of my heart, who so gently marks out the life-
track for me, draw near to-night;
   Forget the wailing of the low-voiced wind:
   Shut out the moanings of the freezing, and the starving,
and the dying, and bend your head low to me:
   Clasp my cold, cold hands in yours;
   Think of me tenderly and lovingly:
   Look down into my eyes the while I question you, and
if you love me, answer me—
                    Oh, answer me!

II.

   Is there not a gleam of Peace on all this tiresome earth?
   Does not one oasis cheer all this desert-world?
   When will all this toil and pain bring me the blessing?
   Must I ever plead for help to do the work before me
set?
   Must I ever stumble and faint by the dark wayside?
   Oh the dark, lonely wayside, with its dim-sheeted ghosts
peering up through their shallow graves!

Must I ever tremble and pale at the great Beyond?
Must I find Rest only in your bosom, as now I do?
      Answer me—
      Oh, answer me!

III.

Speak to me tenderly.
Think of me lovingly.
Let your soft hands smooth back my hair.
Take my cold, tear-stained face up to yours.
Let my lonely life creep into your warm bosom, knowing no other rest but this.
Let me question you, while sweet Faith and Trust are folding their white robes around me.
Thus am I purified, even to your love, that came like John the Baptist in the Wilderness of Sin.
You read the starry heavens, and lead me forth.
But tell me if, in this world's Judea, there comes never quiet when once the heart awakes?
Why must it ever hush Love back?
Must it only labor, strive, and ache?
Has it no reward but this?
Has it no inheritance but to bear—and break?
      Answer me—
      Oh, answer me!

IV.

The Storm struggles with the Darkness.
Folded away in your arms, how little do I heed their battle!

The trees clash in vain their naked swords against the door.

I go not forth while the low murmur of your voice is drifting all else back to silence.

The darkness presses his black forehead close to the window pane, and beckons me without.

Love holds a lamp in this little room that hath power to blot back Fear.

But will the lamp ever starve for oil?

Will its blood-red flame ever grow faint and blue?

Will it uprear itself to a slender line of light?

Will it grow pallid and motionless?

Will it sink rayless to everlasting death?

Answer me—

Oh, answer me!

V.

Look at these tear-drops.

See how they quiver and die on your open hands.

Fold these white garments close to my breast, while I question you.

Would you have me think that from the warm shelter of your heart I must go to the grave?

And when I am lying in my silent shroud, will you love me?

When I am buried down in the cold, wet earth, will you grieve that you did not save me?

Will your tears reach my pale face through all the withered leaves that will heap themselves upon my grave?

Will you repent that you loosened your arms to let me fall so deep, and so far out of sight?

Will you come and tell me so, when the coffin has shut
out the storm?

Answer me—
Oh, answer me !

INFELIX.

WHERE is the promise of my years ;
    Once written on my brow ?
Ere errors, agonies and fears
Brought with them all that speaks in tears,
Ere I had sunk beneath my peers ;
    Where sleeps that promise now ?

Naught lingers to redeem those hours,
    Still, still to memory sweet !
The flowers that bloomed in sunny bowers
Are withered all ; and Evil towers
Supreme above her sister powers
    Of Sorrow and Deceit.

I look along the columned years,
    And see Life's riven fane,
Just where it fell, amid the jeers
Of scornful lips, whose mocking sneers,
For ever hiss within mine ears
    To break the sleep of pain.

I can but own my life is vain
    A desert void of peace ;

I missed the goal I sought to gain,
I missed the measure of the strain
That lulls Fame's fever in the brain,
   And bids Earth's tumult cease.

Myself! alas for theme so poor
   A theme but rich in Fear;
I stand a wreck on Error's shore,
A spectre not within the door,
A houseless shadow evermore,
   An exile lingering here.